How to Build Your
Retirement Dream

Building a Million Dollar Retirement Is Easier Than You Think When You Use the Right Tools

Randy Weikle

Version 3 6/04/2017 Final & Publish

Contents

Introduction

My name is Randy Weikle, and I am a retired U.S. Army Officer. I previously served as Vice President, Government Healthcare Division at Jackson and Coker, which is one of the country's largest privately owned physician's staffing, and placement firms. I was an accomplished physician recruiter and salesman with more than three quarters of a billion dollars in successfully executed government contracts.

I'm currently working on career number three, which is consulting for individuals and companies in Retirement and College Financial Planning. I have chosen to continue to work, even though my retirement savings and government pension would allow me to live a very comfortable life. I feel so strongly that the Boomer Generation, of which I am a card-carrying member, has got to do more to ensure the legacy of our lifestyle for our children and our grandchildren.

I got into the retirement planning business while doing my own retirement planning research. My experience with brokerage agents was bad, and some was worse than that. Their focus was always on what products they could sell to me that would make them the biggest commission. They never looked at my retirement needs. Further, I was looking at a program that would not start for 35 years, and I wanted someone that would participate in the journey with me.

Unfortunately, every other time I spoke to the company that was handling my retirement needs as well as my wife, Susie's, retirement programs, my agent had moved on. I never knew where exactly, but my account was now being handled by someone I had never spoken with, and he / she never had any idea of my financial requirements that had been laid out in previous discussions.

This process became increasingly difficult as both Susie and I progressed through our careers. I had a government pension / retirement program to manage (#1). I am a Disabled Veteran, so I had a VA disability program that was attached to that retirement, as well (#2). The first company I went to work for after retirement from the Army was sold to a second staffing company and it was then merged with a third staffing company in the same year (#3). Unfortunately for me, because of the mechanics of these mergers, my retirement accounts could not be combined until all the time limits put on the mergers had passed. This added an additional retirement account to manage (#4). I had always contributed to my Individual Retirement Account, so that became account (#5).

Added to this ever-expanding dizzying array of options are Susie's accounts. Susie is a Certified Nurse Midwife, currently retired, but she provided support to women in the healthcare arena for almost 30 years. She had an Individual Retirement Account under her Social Security Number (#6 if you are counting), and for a period worked as an independent contractor. We started a SEP, or Self Directed Retirement Program (#7). Finally, after my retirement she joined a practice in Atlanta which offered a 401(k)-retirement program for their employees (#8).

As you can see, this is not what a typical household will ever have to deal with, but it was my burden to bear. But, my plan administrators kept changing, and just explaining this landscape to each successive "advisor" was very wearing on me.

So, I started doing my own research. My college background was in Business Administration, but I had long since been out of school, and life was in the way of getting back to school for additional degrees. That left self-study, which I enjoy far more than going to school. So, I charted a course through the financial industry which included trading, financial planning and money management. My Kindle currently has more than 600 finance books in the index, and my print library has an additional 400+ books.

Susie continues to remind me that I have been trying for 15 years to convert this whole library to digital, because it has been very difficult to house and move. There is an overwhelming amount of literature that you can find in books, journal subscriptions (of which I subscribe to far too many) and newspaper content, as well as the Internet with blogs and advertisements. On any given day, you can find a document that will call a stock a rocket set to ignite, or the biggest goat of all time that should be sold immediately.

I have taken numerous courses from TDAmeritrade as well as The On Line Trading Academy which have provided me with a very broad background into the finance industry. I am also a Licensed Insurance Agent. I have chosen not to take the Stock Broker and Agent certifications, because I will never work for one of these companies. You will understand why as we move through the book.

The information I uncovered from all this individual study had me scratching my head in disbelief.

Statements like

"This can't be true,"

and

"Why did they never tell me this,"

and

"I wish I had known this five, ten, or even twenty years ago,"

and

"My financial picture today could have been radically different, had I known years ago what I have recently discovered,"

Therefore, I'm on a quest to help future generations to find the "yellow brick road", as it were. I want to help them research, understand, and implement a retirement plan that will allow them to retire when they want. This plan is without the support of the Social Security Administration that may or may not be available to future generations, but my plan will still grow to a level with sufficient funds to support their desired lifestyle for them and their families.

In preparation for this retirement journey, I want everyone to use the right tools, to have the right information and adequate background knowledge. In short, to build the retirement program that they dream about.

This book is for anyone who wants to better their retirement outlook. You can be a high-income salesman or executive, a solo business person, a physician or dentist running a solo or group practice, someone still in school, or someone who worries about the future for their child or a grandchild.

You can be working for a company that offers you a 401(k)-retirement program. But it's never too soon to start talking about your retirement, because time can be your best friend, or your worst enemy. The average retirement can now last thirty or more years, so getting this right is extremely important. Getting this retirement program right is the biggest challenge that every single person currently working, or will be working in the future, can accomplish.

The worst possible outcome is to be retired at age 66+ living a quiet, uneventful life, frugally counting pennies. Then you must return to work at age 80, when your retirement savings run out or the government steals it away with the signing of a single legislative initiative. Can you say, "Welcome to Wal-Mart"? Let's hope this will not happen to you if you follow my suggestions in this book.

With that, I'll start into the most common questions I get when discussing an Indexed Universal Life Insurance Policy. There are certainly more, as everyone's circumstances are different; but these questions will give you the foundation necessary to discuss IUL's. I would like to welcome you to the land of Indexed Universal Life Insurance and financial freedom.

Chapter One

What is an Indexed Universal Life (IUL) program?

An Indexed Universal Life Program is often referred to as *the best retirement program that people have never heard of.* It is a retirement account. It is an insurance program. It has been in the tax code since 1985, but more than that, the concept has been around clear back into the earliest days of our country. It allows you act as your own banker, and develop a program that will provide you with life insurance coverage, but in addition you have a personal cash account (your bank) that you can tap into as necessary, to provide cash for large-ticket items.

Only about one in a thousand agents sell this program and there are many reasons for that. The biggest one is that commissions on these policies are very, very low. The agents don't make a lot of money. There are other instruments that are available for retirement planning, advertised by banks and brokerage houses, that will give individual agents a much better commission structure. And, those products will give the companies they work for a "management fee" of up to three to five percent on an annual basis.

This is an important fact to consider when you are watching TV and a commercial for financial planning comes on the screen. Whales jumping, impressive structures built in 3D, stick figure guys on bicycles. All are there to encourage you to participate with their company. In the next decade some 3.5 trillion dollars, will transition from 401(k) programs to IRA's as Boomers retire. The mother-load of all financial gold mines is out there waiting to be recovered. Three to five percent of three trillion dollars is a lot of money going to the bottom line of a bank or brokerage house! They want to help themselves to it by helping you, and they are going to use a spectacular display of advertising genius to help them get to your money.

Now, this money is still not going to find a home at the Boomers' retirement. Boomers will eventually die, and their estates will pass to their heirs. This will give the government a second bite at the retirement savings apple through the probate system. What is left will still need to be managed by the Next Gen crowd, under the watchful eye of the banks and brokerage houses at three to five percent annually. Quite a scheme, don't you think? And you are funding this process and likely didn't even know it.

IUL's are not linked to a bank or a brokerage house; so, the big Wall Street agencies do not stand to gain the commission and management fees I just mentioned. There are about a hundred insurance companies that offer Indexed Universal Life Insurance programs, and they offer widely different options; but all are listed under the Indexed Universal Life Programs. You will find another dizzying group of options and different programs available to you under the broad heading of Indexed Universal Life Insurance Programs. But you must find an agent who specifically understands this program.

Take Away Points

- IUL's are Insurance Policies
- IUL's are Retirement Programs
- IUL's are not sold by Banks or Brokerage Houses
- IUL's are not advertised on TV
- Only a small number of agents and companies offer IUL's to their clients
- IUL's are referred to as "the best retirement program that no one has ever heard of"
- IUL's have existed for a very long time
- The money in IUL's is yours alone and will not be siphoned off to pay commissions and management fees

Chapter Two

Why Do I Need an Indexed Universal Life Policy if I already have a Retirement Account?

As we will discuss in a later chapter, questions like this one are specific to the individual and their needs. However, I would like to discuss some of the factors that would lead everyone to their specific answer.

Let's start with the question of age. If you are old enough that when you opened your IRA or 401(k) you were not offered a Roth option, then you should indeed have an IUL policy. The specific reason concerns taxes on distributions as they come out of the policy when you make a withdrawal. Traditional IRA and 401(k) distributions are all taxed at withdrawal; so, take your account and divide by three. That will be approximately the amount of money that you will be losing to the government if you do not have an IUL in place. As we will discuss in a future chapter, this 33% withdrawal could and most certainly will increase.

If you are young enough to have a Roth retirement program in place, then we need to look at an additional factor and that is employer matching funds. It is, and always will be, a good policy to accept when someone gives you "free" money. I put the word "free" in quotations because it is not truly free. You will have to pay for this benefit in different ways. This concept of matching funds also applies to traditional 401(k) accounts as well. Always take the money and you will never go wrong.

If your employer does not match funds or you do not have a company retirement program, then you should be using the IUL for your retirement needs. Examples of people who should strongly consider this option are members of the military, or others who have a pension program if they don't meet the time-vesting requirements at retirement. They do not have an option for a

401(k) program; so, the IUL gives them an excellent way to save additional money for other program benefits that will also be discussed in future chapters.

Finally, if you do have matching funds, then your contributions to that retirement account should be capped at the dollar level where the matching funds stop. Each company is different here, and you should consult your benefits counselor or Human Relations department if you are unsure of how your specific program works.

There is nothing wrong, and many things right, with having more than one retirement account. As I discussed in my introduction, we as a family have always put the retirement savings payments at the top of our priority list. We have made saving a priority, and have regularly deposited funds to retirement program. In our case, the mechanics of keeping track of these accounts was the biggest headache, but keeping the money flowing into these accounts was never questioned.

Take Away Points

- Traditional IRA and 401(k) programs are taxable
- Roth IRA and 401(k) programs are currently not taxable
- Always take advantage of Employer Matching Funds
- No Matching Funds---Use an IUL policy
- It is OK to have more than 1 Retirement Program in place

Chapter Three

How can you beat the three Retirement Killers: higher taxes, stock market crashes and government interference?

There are several things that keep most of us up at night. The big three: higher taxes, stock market crashes, and government interference.

The potential for higher taxes is certainly a cause for concern. The national debt is at sixteen trillion dollars at this point. It is on everybody's mind, and our elected officials are looking at ways to cover that debt. One of which is raising taxes.

Current tax rates are slightly lower in comparison to where they have been over the past thirty years. The chart below will give you a historical perspective on where they have been and how much higher they can possibly go, without getting into an area that would set a record.

If you evaluate the last election, one of the top three election concerns is the national debt, and the simple way to start to reduce this debt is by raising the tax base for the country. If you were to pose the question to 100 people on the street, "Do you think that taxes will go up in the future"? More than 90% of them would answer "Yes." There is no place for them to go but up.

One of the common points that you will see in more than 90% of the retirement planning books in print; is an assumption that when you retire you will have a lower income, and with that lower income you will place yourself into a lower tax bracket. My discussion with my clients is at odds with this idea. None of those surveyed seem willing to reduce their standard of living to pay lower taxes. They cite many other things that they are interested in doing in retirement such as travel, starting their own business or doing some independent consulting. And these next-generation goals do not allow for a lower tax base at the individual level. My clients tell me that they will find a way to retire on the money they currently have in savings, but they are not going to make the sacrifice of the things that they have looked forward to during their entire working career now that they have reached the age; and financial position where they can begin to check off some of these major bucket-list items.

So, your tax level in retirement will likely remain the same, or go up. That is, unless you have your money in an IUL, which is tax free at the distribution phase. This money is protected from the long arm of the government, now and in the future. Score one big point for the little guys, in their fight to finance their retirement, and retire the way that they want.

Average Federal Tax Rates, by Income Group, 1979 to 2010 and Under 2013 Law

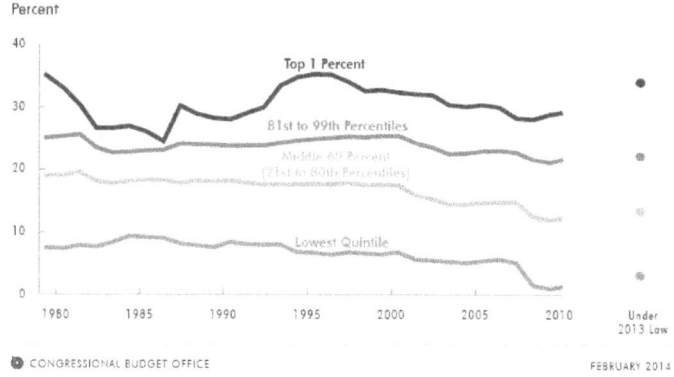

Percent

Top 1 Percent

81st to 99th Percentiles

Middle 60 Percent
(21st to 80th Percentiles)

Lowest Quintile

1980 1985 1990 1995 2000 2005 2010 Under 2013 Law

CONGRESSIONAL BUDGET OFFICE   FEBRUARY 2014

Our second big retirement killer is the stock market. The stock market is always a gamble. It's like rolling the dice. If you look at the period from 2000 to 2009, there were three major adjustments or "crashes" during that time frame. The crash in 2008 reduced retirement incomes in this country by almost forty percent. Moving forward, the probability is that this is going to happen again.

Financial advisors have referred to the last 10 years as the lost decade. When you look at the chart below, you can see that the "crashes" have brought about virtually zero growth. If you add the lost time that 10 years of earnings could have added to your accounts, then you are still significantly behind where you could have been if you were not deeply invested in the stock market.

An additional fact to consider here; if you lose 50% of the money in an account, then a 50% gain in the next year will not recover the entire loss. It takes a 2 x 1 growth rate to replace money lost in a down turn. Consider this example; you have $100,000 in your account and you lose 50%. You now have only $50,000. In the next year, you have a 50% growth on principal, or $25,000, which brings your account to $75,000. It takes a 100% growth i.e. 2 x 1 to recover any losses you sustain.

Zero Growth over this time frame

S&P 500 (1950-2016)

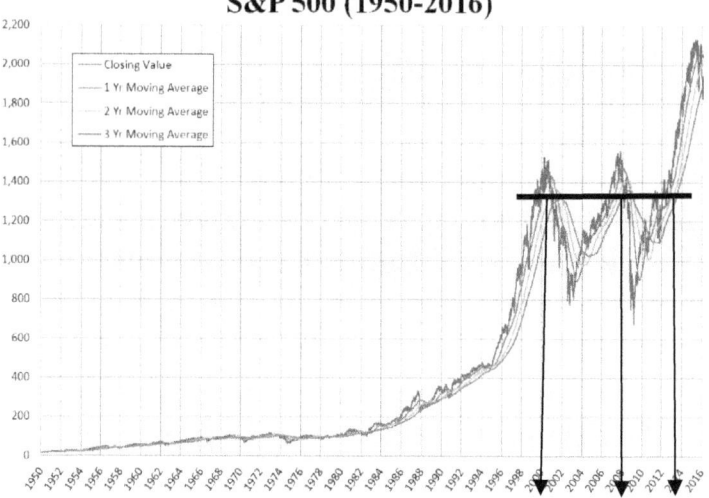

There are many naysayers in the industry that continue to say, "There is another crash coming." Chicken Little is alive and well on all the financial talk shows, and he most likely runs a blog and a well-known chat room.

Finally, the third retirement killer is the government interference probability. The most concerning news / rumor that I read now is the concern that the government has with the national debt. They're looking at how they can tax the tax-free Roth IRA's and Roth 401(k)'s. They can adjust those tax rates with a single legislative initiative. Now they are looking at how they can acquire the money that is in the tax-free programs. I just don't trust the federal government.

I want to look for a retirement program that gets me out of all three of these major concerns; the tax program changes, stock market instabilities, and what our elected officials are going to do to ease the national debt. I think the IUL is the answer to these major concerns.

Take Away Points

- The national debt will have a significantly negative effect on retirement programs
- The probability of taxes going up is high
- Tax rates in retirement will not go down
- There will be future stock market adjustments
- Government interference in retirement programs is inevitable

Chapter Four

How will an Indexed Universal Life Policy help me to not run out of money as I grow older?

Running out of money in your retirement account prior to your death, or, if married the death of both you and your spouse - is perhaps the single biggest concern of aging Boomers. By making use of the ability to withdraw money from the cash value portion of an IUL you can create a long-running cash flow. The cash value portion of the account can be used as a checking account to periodically withdraw money from the policy. This money can be used as a loan, as we will discuss shortly. The exciting fact around this option is that the withdrawals can come from the death benefit that will be paid to your heirs.

In a traditional retirement program, you have a finite level of cash in your account that is limited by how much money has been invested into the account. With an IUL, you can make use of the loan program and tap into the death benefit money that has been set aside for your death. This will, in a sense, allow you to begin to spend your death benefit prior to your death.

The IUL program will make these withdrawals from the maximum death benefit and as necessary reduce that value by the amount of money you have available for distribution. While this will not guarantee that you will have sufficient funds to live the lifestyle that you want and have dreamed about, it will certainly allow you to stretch the available cash for many additional years.

Nothing will substitute for putting sufficient money into your retirement accounts during the growth period of the account. As an example, if you have $200,000 dollars in a traditional account, your balance will decrease each time that you transfer money into your spending accounts.

Within an IUL, once the money has been deposited, that same $200,000 with a 10-year growth period and a death benefit of $1 Million would allow you to make the withdrawals against both the $200,000 and the death benefit of $1Million dollars, giving you a useable balance of $1.2 Million. The principal continues to grow at the rate of your selected index.

See the chart below for a quick example on how much longer an IUL account can extend your withdrawal phase of the policy.

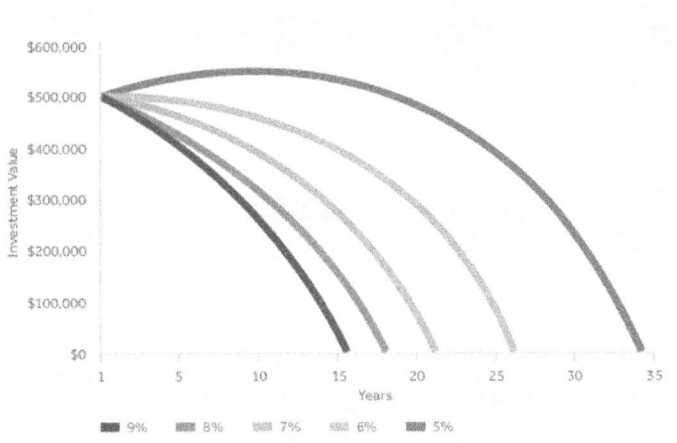

Take Away Points

- The judicious use of the death benefit associated with an IUL will significantly extend the withdrawal phase of the policy
- In simple language, you get significantly more bang for your buck with an IUL

Chapter Five

What are the top five benefits to an Indexed Universal Life Policy?

An IUL program is an individual program, and everybody's top five benefits will be different. The top five benefits for me; - the top five reasons that I have invested in IUL's for myself and my family - may not be the top five benefits that are important for you. What I'm going to address now are the top five benefits that are most often requested by my clients as we set up their programs. In many cases, the other benefits of owning an IUL are hidden benefits that the clients weren't unaware of, and are significant after-thoughts for purchase, but were not involved in the initial decision to put a policy in place.

The first benefit is that the growth and principal amounts when withdrawn from an IUL are not taxable. The government is not involved in the distribution from this policy. Individuals who own an IUL policy will not suffer the same "theft of benefits" as all of us that are currently enrolled in the Social Security Program have experienced. (appendix 1 on the raiding of the Social Security Trust Fund) Simply put, the Social Security Trust Fund was solvent, but government manipulation has caused that solvency to be in doubt.

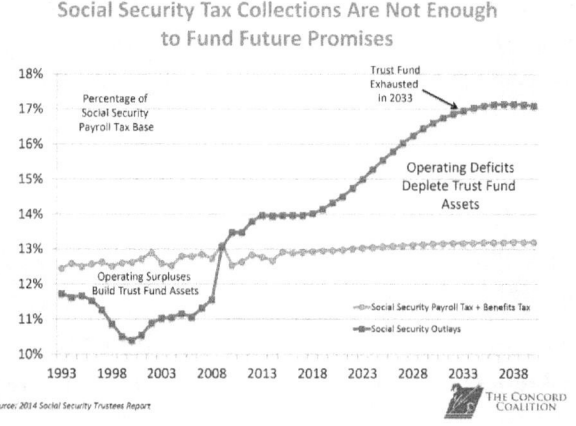

Social Security Tax Collections Are Not Enough to Fund Future Promises

Question number two is "by how much and what can be done about this major problem?"

Currently, the SSA Trust Fund is distributing
more money than it collects each year.

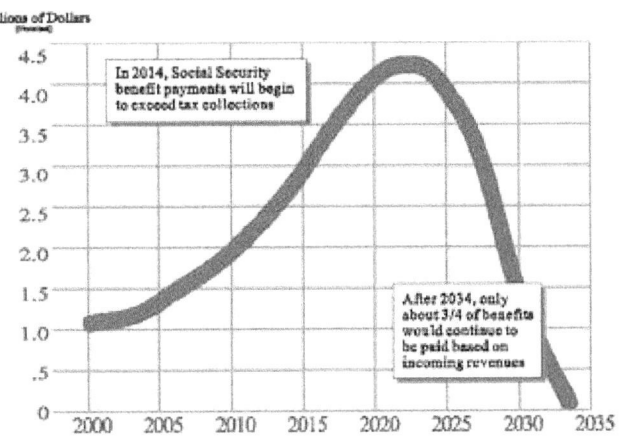

This has been caused by a diversion of funds,
and there are currently not enough workers
contributing to the fund to cover the
distributions.

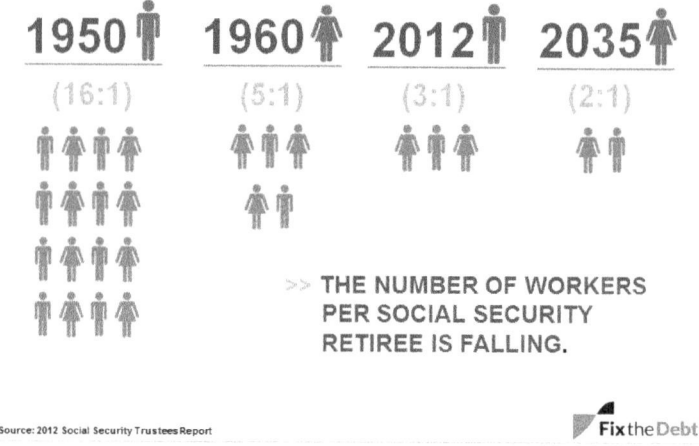

THE POPULATION IS AGING

1950 — (16:1)

1960 — (5:1)

2012 — (3:1)

2035 — (2:1)

>> THE NUMBER OF WORKERS PER SOCIAL SECURITY RETIREE IS FALLING.

Source: 2012 Social Security Trustees Report

FixtheDebt

Compounding this problem, the average American who is supported by this program is living longer, thus drawing benefits for a much longer time than the founding fathers projected when the fund was established. The chart below will help to explain this problem.

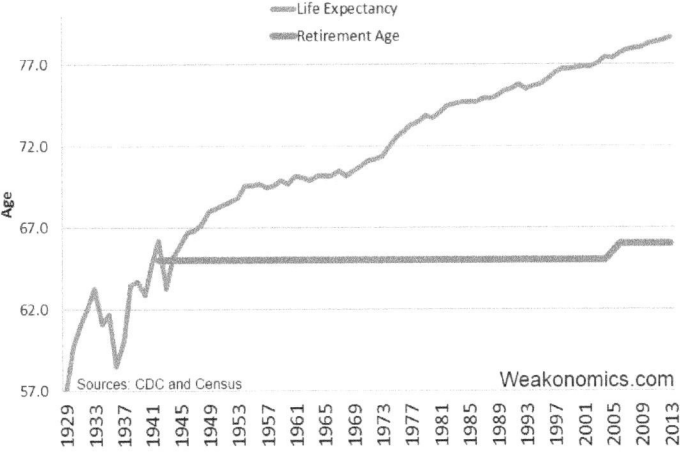

US Life Expectancy and Social Security Retirement Age

Life Expectancy
Retirement Age

Factor number 3 is the death benefit. Many people, when addressing insurance and retirement funding, see these issues as two separate funding items. They contribute to both requirements individually, rather than allowing the IUL to combine these requirements under a single payment.

Benefit number 4: My personal program uses this option that has an interesting twist to make the insurance payment portion of the annual bill slightly lower. My personal policy has a one-million-dollar payout upon the death of both my wife and myself. It's called the "last to die" policy. The death benefit goes immediately to my children when the last member covered under the policy dies. It allows a couple who have differing health risks to combine them under one policy. My beneficiaries will get the death benefit immediately at that point. It does not have to go through probate. It's not evaluated; it's not taxed. The insurance company will send each of my beneficiaries (two sons) a check for money that's in the policy. That would be a minimum of one million dollars split between the two boys, or five hundred thousand dollars each.

Number 5 is the use of the "low or no cost" personal or business loan. We will go into this specific item in Chapter 10 because of the unique and robust problem solving that this feature will allow to the well-informed retirement plan.

Take Away Points

- IUL's are not taxable
- Social Security has many major areas of concern
    - Collections no longer cover expenditures
    - The SSA Trust fund is no longer solvent
    - Working population is too small to support the growing retired population
    - Social Security recipients are living longer
- IUL's have a Death Benefit
- IUL's can be used for business or personal low- or no-cost loans

Chapter Six

Is it true that an Indexed Universal Life Policy will never lose money?

One of the wonderful benefits of this program is that your balance in the account will never lose money over an entire year. All IUL's have this option. Some IUL's will sweeten this pot with a programmed minimum growth rate of one, two, or three percent, and all IUL's will have a programmed minimum growth rate of one, two, maximum of anywhere between thirteen and twenty-five percent. Each one of these programmed minimum growth rate parameters is different based on the company that you will be contracted with. It is important that you understand the policy specifics for your individual policy.

Some of these policies will even give you a "look back" rate in that they will look back over the policy year and compare your chosen index; and if there is a difference, some companies will give you a Mulligan. If the index that you're adjusted against loses money, your policy will not lose money. The chart below is computed based on a zero percent growth program option.

If the stock market does exceptionally well, and your index gains twenty-five percent and your programmed maximum is eighteen percent, you will get the eighteen percent maximum growth.

The chart below looks at how a policy grows over time with no losses and has a maximum growth rate of 15 percent.

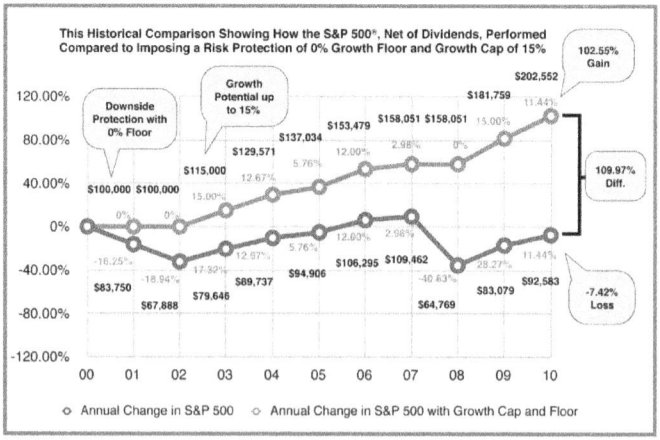

44

I talked previously about the social security trust fund and how the Social Security money was diverted. An IUL program will never suffer this kind of loss. This money is yours and it will never be touched by Uncle Sam.

I recently went through the loss of both my mother and my father in a five-week period. I could move most of their policies through the distribution process without going through probate, in a short period of time. This simplified payment process is a big, big, big, help when you're trying to pay for expenses that accompany the loss of a loved one.

There are no contributions limits to an Indexed Universal Life program.

If you are familiar with the 401(k) programs, the Traditional IRA and the Roth IRA, then you know that these programs have capped maximum policy input. If you're a high-wage earning employee and you want to put money into an account, you are capped at somewhere between five thousand and seventy-five hundred dollars, depending on the current year, contribution limits and your age. Older wage earners are allowed what is called a catch-up contribution, but to my way of thinking it will take you a very long time to "catch-up" if your maximum contribution can only be increased by $1000-$2500 annually.

With an IUL, you can input as much money as you want. Once you cover the life insurance policy requirements, all additional contributions go into the policy cash value bucket that increases the death benefits or can be used in the loan process. Additionally, this portion of the policy offers you great flexibility with your payments. If for some reason, you are unable to make this portion of the payment, there is no penalty associated with the required payment, either up or down. You are free to contribute as your monthly or annual budget allows. At the end of a year when you are looking for somewhere to stash that small nest egg that you were not expecting, it can be used here. If you get a significant commission or a raise at the office, again, this is where you can stash that cash to make a big impact on the family for years to come.

Take Away Points

- IUL's will never lose money
- IUL's have their own variable policy year specific to each individual policy
- IUL's may have a programmed minimum growth rate of 1-2-3% based on the company
- IUL's will have a programmed maximum growth rate
- The Government will not be able to access the money in this account for any reason
- IUL's have no contribution limits
- IUL's have a flexible payment schedule

Chapter Seven

Who can own an Indexed Universal Life Policy?

IUL's are not linked to work status.

Anyone can own an IUL. In my family, my wife and I own an IUL, my single son owns an IUL, my married son owns an IUL, and we have a term rider covering his wife. Both of my grandchildren, who are three and five, have IUL's.

Linking younger people to these policies gives them a significant benefit, in the value of time. This extended time-line allows them a very long growth period for the cash value of the policy. By funding them now, with the "no questions asked" loan program, I can pay for my children's college education or my grandchildren's tuition and expenses for their college education. The potential for purchasing homes for them and the associated down payments is there. The potential to purchase cars without a bank loan is possible, and the potential to cover the expenses for significant family events like weddings without crippling my own retirement savings is secure. Finally, should you have the need to cover extended medical care for your aging parents, the cash is available.

All those things can be taken care of in an IUL policy that was opened for them when they were very young.

Take Away Points

- Anyone can be covered by an IUL
- Earned income is not a requirement to determine ownership
- Age is not a requirement to determine ownership

Chapter Eight

How safe are the companies that offer an Indexed Universal Life Policy?

In looking at these programs there is a difference between an insurance company, a bank or a brokerage house.

Insurance companies look at things over the long term. They look at instruments that are going to be used in twenty, thirty, or fifty years. Banks look at the next quarter, brokerage houses look at the next day, or what's showing up on the stock tickers in the next hour; and so, each has a very different perspective on risk.

The federal government requirements for what they have in their on-hand house assets changes significantly between these three types of companies. Their risk analysis changes based on how much money they can speculate with, and how much must be kept in their reserve accounts.

Banks tend to go out of business. There's never a day that you look at the newspaper, or an investing television show, or even one of the popular weekly or monthly financial magazines, that the stability of a bank somewhere in the world is not being called into question.

In 2008, because of the results of the stock market crash, more than 300 major banks had to close their doors.

The chart below will give you an idea of how big a problem this could be for your retirement program that is going to stretch over a 50-60-year time-frame from origination until distribution to your heirs.

2008 Is a Record Year for Failed Bank Assets

Total Assets of Failed FDIC-Insured Commercial Banks and Savings Institutions by Year, 1988 - 2008*
($ Billions)

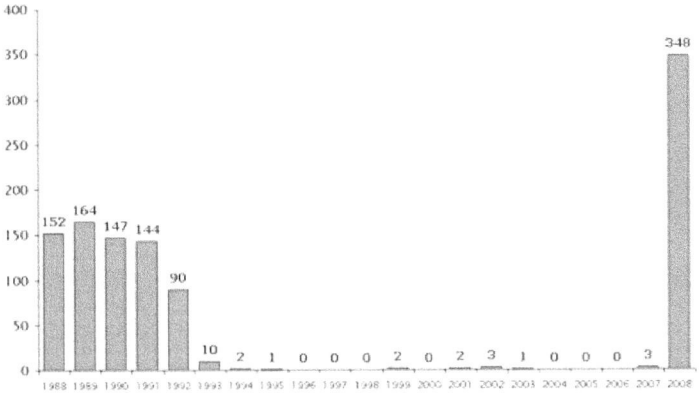

* Through first nine months of 2008.

There were many very large banks and brokerage houses that went out of business and / or declared bankruptcy.

Look at this list of major players on the financial scene that ran into trouble: Washington Mutual, the sixth largest bank in America, collapsed. Wachovia, the fourth largest bank in the country, collapsed. Bank of America, the single largest bank, needed a massive injection of funds from the government to remain open.

Looking at Brokerage Houses:

- **Lehman Brothers** went bankrupt
- Merrill Lynch as well

- AIG went bankrupt
- Bradford & Bingley nearly so
- Fortis nearly so
- Hypo came close to bankruptcy
- Alliance & Leicester also came very close to bankruptcy and had to be rescued.

And "What did this cost the American public?". More than 700 Billion Dollars in just the first round of bailouts.

Looking at the chart below we should have seen this coming, but short-term goals, and no concern for risk management; led the banking industry down the wrong path.

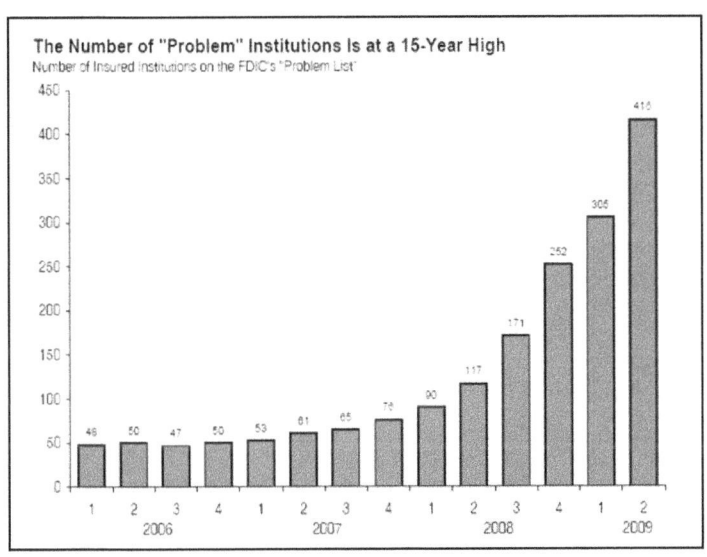

The Number of "Problem" Institutions Is at a 15-Year High
Number of Insured Institutions on the FDIC's "Problem List"

In one hundred and eighty-nine years, there has never been an insurance company that has declared bankruptcy. They have been merged, other agencies have purchased their assets to become bigger or to keep them in business; but there has never been one that has had to declare bankruptcy.

They are the safest form of retirement program that you can buy.

I'm sure that no one has ever said that to you. You certainly don't hear it discussed in commercials on television.

Take Away Points

- Insurance companies are the safest place that you can put money for the long-term requirements of a retirement program
- No insurance company has ever declared bankruptcy.

Chapter Nine

What is tax code 7702?

7702 is the federal government's program for the Indexed Universal Life Program.

It is the location in the tax code that you would look at if you were looking for an IUL.

Since most of us have not read the several hundred thousand pages of the tax code, we hear about the ones that someone has talked to us about.

- If you're employed, it's the 401(k).
- If you work for a non-profit organization it is 403(b).
- Both plans offer a Roth alternative for after-tax contributions.
- If you are self-employed, it is the SEP IRA.
- If you work for the state government you have a 457 or 457(b).

- Then you have the most widely known IRA, or individual retirement account, that is sponsored by the federal government.

What do all these have in common? They are all administered by banks and brokerage houses for a "small" administrative fee. Fees are important when the prize is 3.5 Trillion dollars. That is some $90 Billion dollars annually in "management fees." You see banks and brokerage houses in commercials. Lots and lots of commercials because it takes 7-10 exposures according to the sales gurus of the world before you remember the advertisement.

A 7702 is just another paragraph in the federal government retirement code, but because you would need to substitute "insurance company" for bank or brokerage house, and these companies don't make any money through commissions and management fees, you haven't heard about it.

Take Away Points

- Banks and Brokerage houses manage
  - IRA
  - SEP IRA
  - 401(k)
  - Roth 401(k)
  - 403(b)
  - Roth 403(b)
  - 457
  - 457(b)
- Insurance Companies offer
  - 7702 Insurance Products

Chapter Ten

Can you explain the Loan Program that is part of the Indexed Universal Life Policy?

My guess here is that you are going to love this benefit of an IUL.

You own the cash portion of the account and you can use if for whatever you need in your life.

Think of this as a giant check book that just keeps getting larger as you continue to make your monthly or annual payments into the IUL.

You can now use the money from this account for big ticket items.

- Want to buy a car? …. write a check and then make the payments back to yourself.
- Kids going to college? …. write that check and then, again, make the payments to yourself. If they are going to contribute to your children's or grandchildren's college education, they can make the payments to you, or if you opened an account for them…. they can make the payments back to their own IUL.
- Got a wedding in the future? …payments just became easier.
- Planning a great trip to celebrate an anniversary? Susie and I are going to cruise around the world for our 40th wedding anniversary. Guess how I am going to pay for that trip. Right you are. Thank you, IUL.
- Planning to buy a new house and need a down payment? Want to help the kids buy their first house, but don't want their second mortgage on your credit history? Write that check.
- Want to start a business and get away from the daily rat race? Here is where you find the seed money.

- Do you currently own a business that is in desperate need of some new equipment? Write the check and make your employees happy.

Do you get the picture? You can now become your own banker, approve your own loans as needed, and never must check your credit score again.

Now, with all that money flowing out of the account, the IUL will give you an unexpected benefit that no bank will ever consider. They do not debit your cash account value when they determine their growth for the year. This option is as cool as an option will ever get. The IUL is now giving you a double dip at the well. The money that you have taken out is now doing double duty.

An IUL is generally supposed to be a very low-risk way to save for the future and cover the death benefit for your family. If you are the gambler or stock broker that everyone else wants to be, you can also take that money out of the IUL, invest it in the stock market, reap the windfall (we all hope, anyway) and then put the money back into the IUL with a nice healthy profit.

The final amazing benefit to the loan program is that you have a choice to never pay the loan back at all. That's right, no-payment loans. The IUL sponsoring company will take the loan out of the death benefit when that portion of the account is triggered at your death.

Take Away Points

- IUL loans can be used for any expense that you, the owner, wish to fund
- IUL's are self-approving so no bank approval is required
- You can pay the principal back using a flexible repayment plan
- You can choose to not pay the loan back at all
- This money will perform double duty by covering the original reason for the loan, but still earning interest for your retirement account

Chapter Eleven

Can I really Retire Tax Free?

The answer to that question "Can I retire tax free?" is maybe. If you change the question to "Can I reduce the amount of taxes that I will have to pay in retirement?" then the answer will be a resounding YES!!

It depends on all the income streams that are in your retirement program.

Let's talk about some of these.

Where does your retirement money come from?

- If you receive a pension, which involves a very small segment of the population, then that income stream will be taxable. Companies have been doing away with pensions over time. The simple reason for this, is that they are very expensive for companies, and governments to operate. A quick Internet search will demonstrate how many federal, state and municipal governments are underfunded with respect to their retirement funds.

Pensions are taxable. So, the answer to that one would be no.

- If your money comes from Social Security, a portion of your Social
- Security is taxable. So that portion answer would be no.
- With a traditional 401K, when you take a distribution is taxable. That answer: NO
- A Roth IRA, the answer to the question would be: It's not taxable yet, but the government is looking at that for a way to help cure the debt.
- If you're talking about a Roth 401(k), that is not taxable yet.
- If you're looking at an Indexed Universal Life Policy, it will never be taxable. All the money that you put into that will become yours and it will never be touched by the federal government. Moreover,

when the money is transitioned to your heirs at your death, it will still not be taxable.

So, in answer to the question at the beginning of the chapter is, it depends. Portions of your retirement earnings can be taxed, but more importantly, with proper prior planning and a good financial advisor, portions of your retirement income can come to you and your heirs as untaxed. And that will get you the answer that you are looking for. More money in you accounts at the end of the year.

That question: "Can I retire tax free?" is the question that got me started researching retirement programs in the first place. My goal was to retire tax free. I can't do it because I receive a government pension because of my military service, but most of my money now goes into an IUL, to be withdrawn from that program as tax free.

Finally, before we leave this question, you should be aware of two different options that have been discussed by the federal government to increase the tax dollars they can collect. You should watch for these in the news, as they may have a big impact on your retirement, if the debt ceiling continues to grow as it has in the last decade.

They are:

1. The federal government is considering putting a limit on how much money you can have inside a Roth IRA. The most recent cap was 3 Million Dollars that would remain untaxed, but that was just the starting point for those discussions.
2. The federal government is also looking at how they can tax all the money that is in Roth retirement accounts, regardless of dollar amount.

Take Away Points

- Pensions are taxable
- Traditional 401(k) 's are taxable
- Roth 401(k)'s are not taxable yet
  - There are rules in place to make distributions from a Roth taxable; so, consult an expert.
- IRA's are taxable
- Roth IRA's are not taxable yet
- IUL's will never be taxable

Chapter Twelve

Are there contribution limits to an Indexed Universal Life Policy?

There are not.

This is a big benefit to people who are high-wage earners, people who have their own business, or are highly paid executives and sales staff. 401(k)'s, IRA's, and government programs have an overwhelming number of regulations that are attached to their retirement programs, and, they are changing all the time.

Should you find yourself awake at night and unable to sleep, Google the requirements that come with some of these retirement options:

- How much money you can put in,
- How often you can put it in,
- How much money you can take out,
- How soon you can take out,
- What the penalties are for taking it out,
- Once you hit a certain age you must take it out.
- Has the money been in the account long enough you can have it, but with a penalty?
- How old are you.

These regulations can change on an annual basis, and they are very difficult for the average person to keep current on.

The regulations for an Indexed Universal Life Program, by comparison, are exceptionally easy to keep abreast of. You put in what you want, when you want to. It has a flexible payment program, so that if you say, "I'm going to put in a contribution of one thousand dollars a month," and you come to a month where you cannot make that contribution, it's okay. They are not going to send you a note that says "you missed your payment," because it is your money, your payment schedule and your choice. You can catch up if you want, or you can just keep going. Once you pay for the smallest portion of the policy, the section that covers the life insurance, the rest of it is all personal wishes and you can put in exactly the amount of money that you want.

This program is used by CEO's and wealthy families to pass on their family wealth and fortune to their heirs and next generations.

When you do a little more research, you will discover that Indexed Universal Life Policies are used by banks. Citi bank has 4.5 billion dollars enrolled in Indexed Universal Life Programs. Chase has 9.8 billion dollars of money enrolled in these programs. Wells Fargo has 19.4 billion. There are four thousand banks that have contributed more than 140 billion dollars to these programs.

Who uses them?

The following presidents have had Indexed Universal Life Programs:

- John Fitzgerald Kennedy
- Franklin D. Roosevelt

- William Howard Taft
- William McKinley
- Warren G. Harding

And, more recently, the former Vice President, Joe Biden, also had one.

Who are the wealthy families who pass money through this program:

- The Walt Disney family
- The J. C. Penny family
- The Rockefellers
- The Rothschilds
- Ray Kroc and his family have them.

Some of the Companies who use Indexed Universal Life Policies to cover their own financial concerns are:

- Wal-Mart
- GE
- Comcast
- Johnson and Johnson
- Harley Davidson
- Disney
- Verizon
- 700 of the Fortune 1000 companies.

These companies use Indexed Universal Life Policies.

So, you must ask yourself at some point in time,

"How is it that I have never heard of this program?"

The rich tend to keep this program quiet. Banks can't make management fees off it.

It is best retirement program you've never heard of.

Take Away Points

- IUL's have no contribution limits
- IUL's have flexible payment plans
- IUL's are ideal for
    - High-Income wage earners
    - Solo Business Owners
    - Executives
    - High-Commission Sales Personnel
- IUL's are used by CEO's
- IUL's are used by Corporations
- IUL's are used by Banks
- IUL's are used by Politicians

Chapter Thirteen

Is it true that one size will not fit all clients?

That is a true statement.

Everyone's retirement goals are different.

What you expect out of your retirement is unique. What your partner expects out of his/her retirement is different from what I expect out of mine.

What everyone is willing to contribute to get to their retirement goal is different.

The timeline for each retirement program is different.

So, the program that my company runs uses a financial algorithm that is based on your individual financial history, your individual financial stability, and what your individual perceived notion of your retirement will look like.

We can gather all that information in a one-hour conference and at the end of our fact-finding conference; we will construct a retirement plan that will meet all your goals. You'll be able to walk out of that meeting and say,

"This is exactly what I need to do to hit my retirement mark."

The dollar figure that most people use as their "goal" for a comfortable retirement is currently $1,000,000. We will tell them exactly what they will need to invest over X number of years to be on the right path to meet that goal. Over time, if you decide, as many people currently have determined that $1,000,000 is not sufficient, then a short call to us, some manipulation with your contribution projections and your retirement deadlines can move that figure to $1,500,000 or even $2,000,000. The beauty of the IUL program is that it has an easily adjusted flexibility with all the input variables. You can make those adjustments with a simple phone call.

One group of people who advertise this program call it "The Barefoot Retirement Plan". It is that and more. I encourage you to read the book written by Doyle Shuler, or call or email me and I will be happy to send you a copy.

One size doesn't fit all, but we do an individualized program that allows you to have a specific tailor fit financial retirement program that will enable you to reach your goals, both for yourself and your family.

Take Away Points

- Retirement Accounts are for individuals
- Individual finances and timelines are different
- Expectations are different for each person
- IUL's are dynamic and flexible
- IUL's can change as you change
- IUL's can work for everyone

Chapter Fourteen

What can I do to Fund an Indexed Universal Life Policy?

Finding the money to fund an IUL is not as difficult as you might expect if you think of this as a traditional bill. It is not.

Start by remembering what this program will do for you. It is insurance, but it is also a savings program, and it is very flexible.

Begin simply with: "I just want to get the policy in place immediately so I can get the value of time working for me." Determine a reasonable dollar target that you consider will not overburden your budget now.

Let's work with a dollar value about the size of a monthly car payment, or $300-$350. Remember that you can always overpay the program and change the death benefit once the policy is in place.

Take out a piece of paper and write IUL monthly payment at the top.

Start with your company 401(k). What is the employer maximum limit for which they will provide matching funds? Are you contributing above that amount? If the answer is yes, then take the additional contribution and move it to the IUL funding balance.

Next, are you investing contributions to an IRA in addition to your company retirement program? If the answer is yes, then you should look at the return that you have been getting over the last several years. Has it lost money? Is the return below the IUL historical average of 9.25%? If the answer to this question is yes, then you may consider moving this money to the IUL, or at the very minimum, make this year's contribution to the IUL and not the IRS. Add this amount to your payment sheet.

Do you own your own home? If the answer here is yes, are you comfortable doing a small home equity loan at x% for the returns of an IUL at 9.25%? If it looks like you can pick up 5-6% on the difference between these numbers, then $3,500-4,000 will get you into your IUL for a very small monthly payment.

Do you currently have insurance plans to cover your family? Again, if the answer is yes, can you get better or more coverage through the IUL than you will under your current policy? My personal guess here is that the payments for the IUL will certainly be less than you are currently paying, so if you keep that payment the same you will be getting higher coverage limits, and all the other benefits of the IUL are "free add-on coverage."

What does your current credit card debt look like? Is it possible to take advantage of a special offer from the bank or credit union to combine these accounts into one single payment? If so, you can take the additional cash you have saved in the process and get your coverage started. If you keep this program in place for a year, and at your annual renewal point the credit card balance is below the cash value in the IUL account you can take advantage of the loan offer from the IUL, pay off the credit cards completely and move that payment into your IUL. You become your own banker with this option and start to take advantage of another of the great benefits of an IUL.

Look at savings accounts. What kind of return are you getting from the bank or credit union? My guess is that the 1-2% that they are currently paying will be well below the estimated 9.25% that you will get from the IUL. And again, with the IUL balance, you own this money; so, if you have an emergency your signature will get you the money that you need. And again, as you repay this money, it goes 100% back into your account.

So far, we have addressed options that do not require you to make any adjustments to your current lifestyle. Where are you on the IUL balance sheet you have on the table? Have you found enough to cover your required payment yet? Have you decided that you want to go bigger? Are you willing to forgo some of the small perks you get daily?

Here is a very simple one. Buy a thermos. Fill it before you leave the house with coffee, and skip the morning coffee shop on your way into the office. Monthly savings is more than $100 for 20 cups a coffee at more than $5 per cup. And you may just get an extra 15 minutes of sleep because you have cut out the lines at the coffee shop.

Lunch at the office is on average $15. Brown bag it two or three days a week. Two days a week adds $120 to the monthly total, three days a week brings the amount up to $180.

Willing to do some additional part-time work? It will come back to you several fold, over time.

Look around the house. Having trouble closing the closet or garage door because of all the "stuff" cluttering the space? Then it is time for a garage sale, a trip to the consignment store, or opening an e-bay account and making a little money on the side.

Do you have an unexpected windfall coming your way?   Do you have a tax return coming in? Are you due for a promotion at work, or an annual longevity cost-of-living increase? These events will come with an increase in your monthly income. Divert it to your IUL and you will sleep better.

Take Away Points

- With just a little work and some creativity you can afford an IUL
- Money can come from several different locations
    - Reallocate your current payments
    - IRA funds past, present or future
    - Home equity
    - Convert a current insurance policy
    - Restructure your current debt
    - Move your emergency savings to the IUL
    - Reduce your current expenses
    - Take on some part-time work
    - Look for unexpected windfalls that can pay for your IUL

Chapter Fifteen

I like it, I want it. How do I get an Indexed Universal Life Policy?

This one is simple:
Get in touch with me in any way you can:

Mail:

Randy Weikle
345 Young Harris St.
Suite 430
Blairsville, GA 30514

Email me:

Rweikle2005@gmail.com

Or call me: 678-642-5506

Take Away Points

- We should become great friends over this process. If I can't put the policy in place for you, I will be happy to find an agent who can.

Chapter Sixteen

I need your help to spread the word on Indexed Universal Life Policies!!

I hope that over the course of reading this book, you have discovered that IUL's are an excellent way for everyone to save for the future and help to provide for their families after their death.

If you do a Google search, you will discover very few articles on this policy, and many of these will be negative. We have discussed the reason for this above. Banks and brokerage houses don't like these policies because of the low potential commissions and management fees.

Help me spread the word.

I want to help you.

I want to help your friends.

I want to help the people you work with.

Give them a copy of this book.

Give them my contact information.

Tell them how to get a copy of the book on Amazon.

Please, if you got something out of this book, take 2 minutes and write a review that others can see.

Finally,

I want to thank you for taking the time to read my book.

I hope that you have learned something.

I hope that you enjoyed the process.

I hope you go out and purchase an IUL.

I hope that I have showed you how to build the retirement that you dream about.

Take Away Points

- Please help me spread the work on this great program.

Summary

Those are the sixteen chapters in the book that provide answers to the most frequently asked questions about an IUL. We've looked at each of them and we've looked at some of the amazing offers and benefits that you might find are difficult to believe, much as I did.

- Not taxable
- Government not involved
- Will not be diverted to pay for other government programs
- A death benefit, a no-tax death benefit
- Low- or no-cost loans to cover personal and business expenses

Each one of these benefits is available to everyone who currently has or puts in place an IUL policy.

If you had your money in one of these programs twenty years ago, your potential for retirement would look drastically different than it does today.

If you come in to see me, you will get to see our

On the Mark, Tailored, Never Miss Retirement Action Program Analysis

This analysis will give you a custom plan that highlights your specific retirement needs, based on your financial position. We will provide you with a step-by-step plan to go from your current age, to your desired age at retirement, and what you're going to have to do financially, in each of those years, to meet that plan.

The financial projection will give you an annual milestone that will confirm that the program is on pace, or to show you how you must make small corrections that will allow you to reach that goal.

Finally, you'll have a sense of well-being and know that you'll be working with people who have your interests at heart.

Commissions are not paid by you in this program. We are here strictly to help you establish your account.

Give me a call.

My phone number is 678-642-5506,

You can reach me at my website.

www.redzoneretirementplanning.com

I will be happy to assist you in any of the states that revolve around

Georgia,

Florida,

Alabama,

 North Carolina,

South Carolina, and

Tennessee.

I have been known to add additional state licenses to assist clients that are out of my current territory. I want to help you.

 My goal is to help you establish an IUL retirement program.

From me to you, your family and your loved ones, Thank you.

Appendix 1

Has Social Security (Ever) Been "Raided"?

20 Sep 2010
By Eric Laursen

Social Security is always being raided. And some brave person – typically an elected official or someone aspiring to be – is always vowing to stop this outrage before our retirement system is drained to the dregs. That's just how it is in mad as hell America, where righteous indignation comes slickly packaged and accurately defining one's terms is an unnecessary formality.

"Don't raid Social Security to reduce nation's deficit," pleads the AARP. Meanwhile, right-wing gold bugs are warning us that a "huge pot of U.S. Social Security money" is "vulnerable to being tapped by illegal alien workers." And over on Capitol Hill, intrepid Sen. Jim DeMint promotes a "Stop the Raid" amendment, protesting that "It's time for politicians to stop stealing from our seniors to secretly finance trillions in wasteful Washington spending."

The Great Social Security Raid has become the Sasquatch of American politics: the creature that's always out there but never clearly seen, the monster just under our noses or just beyond our field of vision. We think we know it's there. But everyone uses the same word to describe something different.

Let's see if we can chase this thing down. First, no one talked about a "raid" until the trust funds began to grow into a substantial amount pool of assets following the 1983 Amendments to the Social Security Act. Critics then began to complain that the trust funds had been "raided" because after using most of our payroll taxes to pay benefits to the current crop of retirees, survivors, and disabled, the Treasury Department borrows the remainder to use for whatever else it damn well pleases, sticking workers with a fistful – actually, a file cabinet - full – of IOUs.

Another way to look at the transaction, however, is that the Social Security trust funds use the money left over after benefits are paid to buy

Treasury Bonds. Either the "assets" in the trust funds are worthless chits, or they are the safest investment in the world. But the excess tax revenues must be invested in something.

Critics of Social Security like to point out that the Treasuries in the Social Security trust funds aren't like the ones individuals or the Bank of Japan buy, because they're not negotiable. The trustees can't turn around and sell them to some other investor. Effectively, one part of the federal government – the Social Security system – has made a loan to another part – the Treasury. That's not "real" investment, that's a shell game. Or, stretching the definition, a raid.

The problem is that the commitments behind those Treasury bonds are legally just as enforceable as the ones that trade on the open market. Social Security receives interest on them. As soon as Social Security needs the money back to pay some of the benefits it owes, the Treasury is obliged to redeem them at full value (it's been doing so this year, in fact, since the recession pushed payroll tax collections below the level needed to pay all current benefits). To not do so would be just as serious a legal breach as to change the terms of the deal on the bonds in the Bank of Japan's vaults. Until that happens, there's been no raid.

Often, what the critics really mean when they talk about a Social Security "raid" isn't that something's been stolen, but that they don't like how those payroll taxes receipts have been invested. Safe and sound as they may be, Treasuries aren't "real" investments, which would be in private sector instruments like stocks and corporate bonds. But according to the critics, if the assets are to be invested in private company securities, this shouldn't be done through the trust funds, which are ultimately controlled by the presidential appointees on the Social Security's board of trustees. As Alan Greenspan once put it, "even with Herculean efforts, I doubt it would be feasible to insulate, over the long run, the trust funds from political pressures."

So here we have yet another form of "raid": a culture of corruption growing up around the trust fund's investments. The only way to prevent it, according to free market fans, is to give individual workers the right to investment some portion of their payroll taxes in the form of private accounts. The raid can only be stopped, in other words, if the money is given back to the people who paid it in.

But wouldn't that lead to yet another kind of raid? Most privatization proposals wouldn't give the people their money back. They'd be given the choice of allocating their payroll tax dollars between a select group of investment vehicles, all run by prominent financial services firms. Is the purpose here to help working people earn a higher return on their investments? Or is it to prop up an overvalued stock market – and provide Wall Street with the steady, fee based incomes it needs to cushion its high stakes gambling – er, trading – desks? If the latter, then who's doing the raiding?

OK, let's get realistic. If by "raid" we simply mean that Washington has been able to "use" our payroll taxes for something other than supporting Social Security, then there might be a case to be made. The Reagan administration famously used the hike in payroll tax receipts in the 1980s – which was already scheduled in the 1977 Amendments, Reagan and Congress just moved the dates up – to compensate for the tax cuts he'd pushed through in 1981, and which had ballooned the deficit. Since then, ordinary workers' payroll taxes have essentially been used to pay for tax cuts for the affluent.

But even this stretches the definition of a "raid." Those payroll taxes are still used to purchase Treasury bonds. It's the proceeds from these that cushion the federal budget from the impact of income tax cuts for the upscale. They could be used for something else – education, green energy initiatives, antipoverty programs, etc. – and the Treasuries in the trust funds still must be redeemed. If the trust funds are going to invest in Treasuries, Congress is going to do something with that money. It's not going to sit on it.

The real discussion, then, needs to be about whether Congress is using the proceeds from those Treasury in ways help the economy to grow. But this is never really addressed in the Discourse of the Raid, which most often obscures the fact that the assets in the trust funds have been invested, not stolen. Social Security – and the pool of assets that supports it – are the property of the working Americans who pay into it.
Do we want our money to be invested in tax cuts for the holders of capital?

Wars in the Mideast?
Charter Schools?
Health Care?

If the Treasuries in the trust funds are redeemed
– if the federal government honors the
covenants behind the bonds – there's no raid.
Except, perhaps, for one thing:

Suppose Congress decides to cut Social Security
benefits. Cutting benefits, absent a
corresponding cut in payroll tax rates, would
mean that less of the trust fund assets are needed
to pay benefits. That would lower the required
rate of redemption on those Treasury bonds.
And that would mean more of the money from
those bonds stays in the hands of Congress for a
longer period to spend as it pleases.

That would be playing fast and loose with the
social compact represented by the Social
Security trust funds. Workers who had paid into
the system for years under one set of
expectations could now look forward to getting
much less for their money. And that, in a sense,
would be a raid.